What Experts Are Saying

"This book is an excellent reference/guidebook for leadership in any size organization. I found myself taking notes and wanting to apply the concepts to my business from the very first chapter. I will be recommending this book to my clients, from start-up businesses to companies that are seasoned and successful."
—Douglas M. Marshall, III CPA

"...Daphne diagnoses the reality beneath the surface of organizational life; she prompts leaders to bring their divergent styles and views out into the open so they can tackle conflict directly and reach alignment; and she demonstrates how equity and top performance are mutually reinforcing values."
—Dr. Olivia A. Golden, former nonprofit ED and senior public sector leader

HUMAN CAPITAL

AT THE

CORE

Strategies for Sustainable Workforce Transformation

DAPHNE B. LATIMORE

Paperback ISBN: 979-8-9995436-0-8
Hardback ISBN: 979-8-9995436-1-5

Published by

The Publishing Pad
www.thepublishingpad.com

Table of Contents

Foreword

By **Jackie Hilton**,
Senior HR and People/Culture Professional

There has never been a more urgent time to rethink how we build, grow, and sustain the people side of our organizations.

We're navigating a complex workplace landscape—one where expectations are evolving, agility is no longer optional, and people want to work in environments that are not only high-performing but also human. In the midst of these shifting dynamics, the role of people leaders has expanded. We're not just stewards of process; we are architects of culture, catalysts for equity, and strategic partners in transformation.

That's why this book matters.

In *Human Capital at the Core: Strategies for Sustainable Workforce Transformation*, Daphne Latimore brings forward the clarity and courage we need to evolve. She doesn't just talk about the importance of culture or the need for engagement—she shows us how to operationalize those values through systems, behaviors, and leadership alignment.

This is not a book filled with abstract theory. It's grounded in decades of real-world experience working across sectors, guiding complex change, and helping organizations move from intention to action. Daphne has a rare ability to cut through the noise and get to the heart of what drives transformation: behavior, accountability, and people-centered leadership.

What I appreciate most about her approach is that it affirms something we all know to be true but sometimes forget: HR is not just a function—it's a force. And when done well, it has the power to shape not only careers but cultures.

If you are a Chief People Officer, an HR Business Partner, a senior leader, or simply someone who cares about the future of work, this book will equip you. It will challenge you. Most importantly, it will remind you that sustainable transformation doesn't begin with new software or policies. It begins with how we show up, how we lead, and how we put people at the center of everything we build.

I'm proud to call Daphne a colleague and a respected thought partner in this space. Her work reflects the kind of leadership our organizations need today—and this book is a valuable guide for anyone ready to lead what's next.

Jackie Hilton

Preface

In today's evolving workplace, organizations face a growing tension: the pressure to be agile, inclusive, and performance-driven—all at once. As workforce expectations shift and business models become more complex, many leaders struggle to move from intention to execution when it comes to cultivating strong, sustainable people strategies.

Over the past thirty years, I've had the privilege of supporting a range of organizations—from mission-driven nonprofits and public agencies to large private-sector enterprises—helping them navigate the complexities of workforce transformation. What I've learned is this: HR is not just a function. It's a force. A well-aligned human capital strategy, embedded across the employee life cycle, can become the very engine of organizational health, adaptability, and innovation.

My work sits at the intersection of organizational development and talent management—two disciplines that are often siloed, but when integrated, unlock the full potential of people and culture. Over the past three decades, I've helped leaders and teams align values, systems, behaviors, and outcomes in ways that drive meaningful change.

This book draws from that experience. It's a practical, thought-provoking guide for anyone who shapes culture and leads people—from CHROs and executive leaders to team coaches and OD professionals. Human Capital at the Core isn't just about managing change—it's about redefining success by placing people strategy at the center of business strategy. For too long, HR was seen as the operational backbone—focused on policy, compliance, and administration. But the demands of today's workplace require more than structure; they require strategy. That's where I've focused my work: helping organizations move from intention to execution by aligning leadership, systems, and behavior to create sustainable growth and human-centered impact.

This book reflects the shift from traditional HR toward a more dynamic space, where organizational development and talent management are core drivers of business transformation.

Let's move beyond one-size-fits-all solutions and start building workplaces where equity, performance, and trust are not in competition—but in concert.

Rethinking the Value of Human Capital

"We've checked all the boxes, but something still isn't working."

It's a refrain I've heard more times than I can count. The policies are in place. The performance management system is live. Diversity statements are posted. Engagement surveys have been conducted. And yet—teams are stuck. Morale is uneven, trust is eroding, and leaders aren't sure how to move forward.

This is what happens when human capital is treated as a set of tools rather than a living, evolving system.

In this chapter, we begin by examining the fundamental shift required to lead workforce transformation in today's world: moving from process-centered HR to people-centered strategy.

For too long, organizations have tried to drive performance by managing outputs. But performance is a product of behavior—and behavior is shaped by culture, leadership, and trust.

The Limits of Traditional HR

HR has historically been asked to reduce risk, standardize policies, and ensure compliance. These functions are critical, but they are not sufficient. Processes can help people do their work, but they don't necessarily help people do their *best* work. And they rarely inspire people to remain engaged, loyal, or innovative.

Human capital strategy takes a different view. It centers on the individual—not just as a worker, but as a contributor, a collaborator, and a culture carrier.

Defining Human Capital Strategy

Human capital strategy is more than workforce planning or succession charts. It is a deliberate effort to align talent, culture, and behavior with the evolving needs of the organization. It asks:

- What kind of culture does our strategy require?
- What behaviors do we need to see more of?
- How do we equip, trust, and empower people—not just manage them?

When strategy and culture are aligned, people don't just meet expectations—they elevate them.

The People Function: Reframing the Role of HR

HR must evolve into *the people function*, a center of strategy and insight. This requires HR and OD professionals to think beyond programs and begin designing for experience—because the experience shapes the behavior, and behavior drives outcomes.

This is the work behind the work. And it means asking different questions:

Instead of asking:	"Are people attending training?"
Ask:	"Are we seeing different behavior on teams?"

Instead of asking:	"Do we have a process?"
Ask:	"Do people trust the process—and the people leading it?"

Instead of asking:	"What's broken?"
Ask:	"What's missing from the human capital equation?"

A Living, Breathing System

Your workforce is not a machine to be fixed. It is a living, breathing system of human beings who are responding to what they see, feel, and hear. If the strategy says "Collaborate" but the behaviors reward silos, people believe behavior. If the organization values inclusion but leadership is unclear on what that means day to day, people believe behavior.

To transform the workforce, we must start with behavior. That means intentionally shaping experiences, rituals, leadership actions, and accountability structures so they are grounded in trust and clarity—not just performance expectations.

Case in Point: When the Culture Said One Thing, but the System Said Another

A midsized organization I worked with had recently undergone a strategic shift. The new CEO wanted to foster cross-functional collaboration and innovation. The messaging was clear: "We win as one team."

But when I was brought in to observe leadership behaviors and assess workforce alignment with the new strategy, something was immediately apparent: the structure and culture still rewarded individual competition over collaboration. Leaders' performance was measured on siloed KPIs, teams operated in parallel rather than intersecting, and the team members recognized as high performers were those who stayed in their lane and protected their turf.

In one meeting, a manager said: "I'm all for collaboration—but if I share this resource with another department, my team takes the hit. That doesn't make sense under our current system."

It wasn't that people didn't want to collaborate. It was that the system wasn't aligned with the new strategy. Behavior was being shaped by outdated reward structures and unspoken norms—not vision statements.

Our work began with a simple principle: behavior follows design. We coached leaders to model the desired behaviors, revised incentive structures to reward shared success, and created cross-functional projects with joint accountability.

Six months later, collaboration wasn't just a goal—it was becoming the norm.

Key Takeaway

You can't shift culture with messaging alone. People respond to what's rewarded, who's promoted, and what behaviors are tolerated or reinforced.

Practitioner Reflection Points

- Where is your organization overly focused on process and under-invested in people?
- What behaviors are being reinforced by your current systems—even unintentionally?
- How are you measuring success: by compliance or by culture?

Chapter 1 Summary

- Traditional HR approaches that focus on processes and compliance can limit organizational potential.
- ***Human capital strategy*** centers on people as dynamic contributors whose behaviors drive performance and culture.
- Sustainable workforce transformation requires aligning culture, leadership behaviors, and business strategy.
- HR must evolve into ***the people function***, a strategic partner that designs experiences to shape desired behaviors.
- Behavior follows design. When systems and incentives are misaligned, culture and strategy suffer.
- Transformation starts with intentional leadership actions, clear accountability, and trust-based relationships.

Behavioral Drivers of Performance

Performance doesn't start with metrics.
It starts with behavior.

Every leader wants results, but not all know how to build the behaviors that sustain results. Performance management systems often focus on outcomes—what gets done—without examining the how. Yet it's behavior, more than intention, that determines how teams operate, how leaders show up, and how trust is built or broken.

What drives behavior? Values, expectations, and—most importantly—culture.

When organizations fail to define and model the behaviors they want to see, they leave room for inconsistency, confusion, and disengagement. But when behaviors are clear, aligned, and reinforced, accountability grows. Clarity becomes culture.

Data from the Society for Human Resource Management (SHRM) reveals that unresolved behavioral issues—such as poor communication, disrespect, and avoidance—are among the top reasons employees disengage, leave, or underperform. The root problem often isn't lack of skill; it's lack of behavioral alignment.

Organizations that succeed long-term are those that intentionally identify, model, and reinforce the behaviors that support their strategy.

The Cost of Ignoring Behavior

Behavioral misalignment has measurable costs:

- Increased attrition due to unresolved conflict or unclear expectations.
- Decreased engagement when high performers see toxic behavior tolerated.
- Ineffective teamwork when communication norms are inconsistent.
- Lost productivity when people focus on navigating culture instead of doing their work.

Yet many organizations overlook this cost because behavior is harder to quantify than outcomes. But make no mistake—behavior is the most critical predictor of performance sustainability.

Common Behavior Challenges in Organizations

Behavior Gap	How It Shows Up	Impact On Culture
Avoidance of conflict	Silent meetings, passive resistance	Misalignment, confusion
Inconsistent feedback	Surprise during reviews	Distrust, disengagement
Hero culture	Rewarding "putting out fires" over good planning	Burnout, decreased collaboration
Low accountability	Missed deadlines without follow-up	Team tension, lowered standards

Case in Point: Coaching for Culture, Not Just Compliance

A midsized client engaged me to "fix" their performance review process. They were convinced the form was the issue. But after conversations and observations, the real problem became clear: people didn't know what behaviors mattered. Managers avoided feedback. Teams lacked a shared definition of excellence.

We rebuilt their behavioral competencies, embedded coaching into their performance cycle, and trained leaders to lead with consistency and clarity. The result? Employees were no longer surprised by their evaluations, and managers began using reviews to grow, not grade.

Practitioner Reflection Points

- Are behaviors clearly defined and integrated into your performance systems?
- Do your leaders coach behavior or only manage results?
- What behaviors are tolerated, and what does that say about your culture?
- Are employees recognized more for how they work or just what they achieve?

Chapter 2 Summary

- Behavior—not just output—is the foundation of performance.
- Without shared behavioral expectations, accountability suffers and culture fractures.
- Leaders must be behavior coaches, not just task managers.
- Performance systems must reflect and reinforce the behaviors the organization values

CHAPTER 3

Leadership Alignment: The Culture Multiplier

When leaders are misaligned, culture becomes chaotic. When they're aligned, culture becomes a force multiplier.

In fast-moving environments, even strong leaders can unintentionally pull in different directions. One leader encourages open dialogue; another avoids conflict. One prioritizes collaboration; another rewards individual output. The result? Mixed messages. Misaligned behaviors. Cultural confusion.

Why Alignment Matters

Leadership alignment isn't about unanimity—it's about unity of purpose and behavior. It ensures that:

- Teams receive clear, consistent messages.
- Decisions reinforce shared goals and values.
- Accountability is understood across functions.
- Trust is built through predictability and clarity.

Without alignment, departments create their own microcultures. Performance becomes uneven, communication breaks down, and culture erodes from within.

The Knowledge–Behavior Gap

Most leadership teams don't lack knowledge. They know what "good" leadership looks like, at least in theory. The gap is in behavior—particularly when pressure builds.

Under stress, leaders tend to default to their own preferences or past experiences rather than to agreed-upon norms. That's where alignment breaks down. The ability to lead consistently and visibly through values—especially in moments of tension—is the true marker of leadership maturity.

This is why organizations must go beyond competency models and job descriptions. They must foster behavioral clarity: What does "respect" look like in meetings? What does "accountability" sound like in a coaching conversation? Alignment is a behavioral agreement—not just a strategic one.

Case in Point: Rebuilding Trust Through Alignment

I worked with a newly merged organization where two legacy leadership cultures clashed. One was highly hierarchical; the other was informal and collaborative. Employees reported frustration, burnout, and fear of reprisal depending on which leader they worked under.

We facilitated a leadership alignment process—not to homogenize leadership styles but to create shared behavioral guardrails. Together, the team defined how they would model core values through feedback, recognition, decision-making, and team communication.

The result was a clear behavioral charter. Six months later, engagement scores stabilized and cross-functional collaboration increased. Leaders were no longer working in silos—they were showing up with unity.

Reinforcing Culture Through Experience

Culture is shaped not by what's posted on the wall but by how leaders behave in key moments:

- When conflict arises, do leaders protect? Avoid? Or do they engage to constructively resolve it?
- When feedback is needed, is it delayed? Indirect? Disrespectful? Or is it delivered promptly, directly, and respectfully?
- When someone underperforms, is coaching applied? Or is compliance merely enforced?

Every one of these moments becomes a cultural signal.

Employees learn what matters based on what's rewarded, what's tolerated, and what leaders walk past. This is why sustained leadership alignment is a culture multiplier. When behaviors are consistent, culture becomes self-reinforcing.

Three Anchors for Sustained Leadership Alignment

1. Shared Behavioral Standards

Alignment doesn't mean every leader is the same—it means every leader honors the same expectations in how they lead.

2. Consistent Reinforcement

Recognition, feedback, and accountability must be applied equitably. If one leader overlooks disruptive behavior while another addresses it, trust falters.

3. Feedback at the Leadership Level

Leaders must create space to assess how they are showing up, not just what they deliver. Regular 360° reviews, pulse checks (also called employee engagement surveys), and peer reflections create accountability.

Practitioner Reflection Points

- How aligned are your leadership behaviors across functions or levels?
- When pressure rises, do your leaders reinforce values—or revert to habit?
- Are cultural expectations modeled by leadership or merely stated?
- What's one behavior your leadership team needs to recalibrate?

Chapter 3 Summary

- Leadership alignment either amplifies or erodes culture—there is no neutral.
- When there's misalignment at the top, confusion cascades throughout the organization.
- Leadership behavior, whether consistent or inconsistent, is the clearest culture signal an employee receives.
- Culture is reinforced by the experiences leaders create, not by policy.
- When leaders align not just around strategy but around behavior, they multiply culture.

Designing Systems That Support Accountability

"Every system is perfectly designed
to get the results it gets."
—*W. Edwards Deming*

One of the most overlooked sources of behavioral misalignment is the system itself—the policies, processes, and incentives that shape how people act. Even the most well-intentioned behaviors will falter if they clash with how success is defined and rewarded.

Systems Drive Behavior

Organizational systems silently shape behavior every day:

- Performance review structures that reward individual output over collaboration.
- Incentive programs that prioritize short-term gains over long-term strategy.
- Promotion criteria that overlook soft skills in favor of technical prowess.
- Decision-making hierarchies that discourage initiative.

If your systems are misaligned with your values and desired culture, they'll consistently produce behaviors that conflict with your goals.

Behavioral Alignment as Design Strategy

Behavior-aligned design means engineering your systems to reinforce the culture you want, not just the tasks you need completed. This includes:

- Revisiting job descriptions to reflect behavioral expectations.
- Evaluating performance systems for equity, inclusion, and clarity.
- Embedding feedback loops into the flow of work.

- Training managers to lead behavior conversations, not just task check-ins.

The Role of Leadership and HR

Leaders and HR professionals must be system designers—not just enforcers. They need to:

- Challenge legacy processes that no longer serve the culture.
- Co-create systems with employees to ensure buy-in.
- Regularly audit how systems shape behavior (and misbehavior).

Culture isn't a slogan—it's a byproduct of the systems you build.

Case in Point: Redesigning Performance to Reinforce Belonging

A professional services firm was struggling to meet its DEIB goals despite robust messaging. A closer look revealed that promotion decisions were being made behind closed doors, with little transparency or feedback.

By shifting to a behavior-based performance model—including inclusive leadership metrics and structured feedback loops—the organization saw improved retention, more equitable promotions, and a measurable shift in culture.

Practitioner Reflection Points

- What behaviors are your current systems rewarding—or discouraging?
- How often do you review performance and recognition practices for cultural alignment?
- What systems could you redesign to better reflect your values?

Chapter 4 Summary

- Organizational systems are powerful behavior shapers.
- Misaligned systems produce misaligned behavior.
- Designing for behavioral alignment requires intentional shifts in how success is defined, measured, and rewarded.
- HR and leadership must act as system architects to build cultures where values come to life.

The Engagement–Culture Connection: Turning Beliefs into Behaviors

Culture isn't what's posted on the wall—it's the understood behaviors people exhibit daily, reinforced by what leadership consistently models, tolerates, and rewards.

Organizational values are everywhere: painted on conference room walls, printed in onboarding packets, and embedded in brand statements. But in too many workplaces, values remain aspirational declarations rather than behavioral standards. This disconnect breeds cynicism, inconsistency, and missed opportunities.

Culture vs. Engagement: A Crucial Distinction

Many leaders mistakenly use the terms *culture* and *engagement* interchangeably, but they are not the same.

- ***Engagement*** is how people feel about the organization—their commitment, enthusiasm, and emotional connection to their work.
- ***Culture*** is how people behave in the organization—the unwritten rules, habits, and norms that guide actions.

You can have a highly engaged workforce that still operates in a toxic or misaligned culture. Likewise, you can have a strong, healthy culture where engagement is temporarily low due to external pressures.

What do engagement and culture have in common? Both are enhanced by values-driven behavior. When values are lived consistently, both culture and engagement improve sustainably.

From Words to Workflows

Values are only as powerful as their presence in everyday decisions, conversations, and systems. When values are activated—when they show up in behavior—they become a competitive advantage.

Values activation happens when:

- Leaders model the values consistently.

- Teams use values as decision filters.
- Recognition reinforces value-aligned behavior.
- Misalignment is addressed—not ignored.

When this alignment exists, values guide culture and performance with clarity.

The Cost of Dormant Values

Organizations with misaligned, neglected, or otherwise dormant values face:

- Confusion and disengagement.
- Fragmented decision-making.
- Inconsistent leadership behavior.
- Difficulty navigating change and crisis.

In contrast, companies that actively live their values report stronger trust, resilience, and employee commitment—even during periods of uncertainty.

Activating Your Organization's Values

Values activation requires embedding principles into people systems and daily practices:

- Hiring: Use values-based interview questions to assess alignment.
- Onboarding: Teach not just what the values are but what they look like in action.

- Performance management: Evaluate how work gets done, not just outcomes.
- Recognition: Reward behaviors that reinforce values—publicly and frequently.
- Leadership development: Coach leaders on modeling the organization's stated beliefs, and hold them accountable for this modeling.

Without intentional activation, values become just another branding exercise. With it, they serve as a cultural compass.

The Role of Behavior-Based Culture Assessment Tools

A well-designed culture assessment platform goes beyond measuring how people feel—it looks at how they behave. Rather than relying solely on engagement or satisfaction surveys, behavior-based tools offer a more actionable lens by examining how individuals operate within the organizational system.

These tools help leaders explore questions such as:

- Are team dynamics fostering collaboration or competition?
- Do communication patterns encourage transparency or confusion?
- How aligned are everyday decisions with the organization's stated values?

- Are people empowered to act, or are they waiting for permission?

By measuring behavioral norms—what people do, tolerate, and repeat—organizations can gain a clearer view of cultural health. This type of insight allows leaders to move beyond assumptions and address the root causes of misalignment, disengagement, or inertia.

When behaviors are measured and made visible, leaders can reinforce the practices that strengthen trust, performance, and alignment, and begin shifting those that do not.

Case in Point: Making Values the Standard, Not the Slogan

A professional services firm had strong stated values—integrity, collaboration, and accountability—but frequent complaints about inconsistency in leadership behavior. Mid-level managers reported feeling like "values didn't apply to senior leadership."

The firm partnered with me to implement the Culture15 platform. The assessment revealed wide gaps between declared values and lived behaviors, particularly in decision-making and information flow.

Leadership responded by revising performance reviews to include behavior-based assessments, launching peer-nominated recognition programs, and introducing "values check-ins" at team meetings. After one year, engagement rose by 14%, but more importantly, cross-functional trust and collaboration visibly improved.

Practitioner Reflection Points

- Do your team members know what your values look like in action?
- Where in your organization are values consistently modeled? Where are they ignored?
- How do you recognize and reward value-aligned behaviors?
- Are you measuring behavior—or just sentiment?

Chapter 5 Summary

Engagement and *culture* are related but distinct. One is how people feel; the other is how they act.

- Values matter only when they influence daily behavior.
- Dormant values weaken culture, trust, and strategic clarity.
- Tools such as Culture15 can help organizations measure behaviors and shift them toward alignment.
- *Values activation* requires leadership modeling, operational alignment, and constant reinforcement.

Trust, Belonging, and the Equity Mindset

Inclusion isn't a program—it's the everyday experience of being valued, respected, and given equal opportunity to contribute and grow, regardless of who's in the room.

The conversation around equity, inclusion, and belonging has evolved. What was once treated as a compliance function or a standalone program is now recognized as central to culture and business performance. However, for many organizations there remains a disconnect between intention and impact.

True inclusion is not a destination—it's a cultural capability. It requires embedding equity into the way people are hired, developed, evaluated, and led.

Culture Work, Not Just Engagement Work

Many organizations confuse engagement efforts with culture building. But, as discussed in the previous chapter, engagement is about how people feel at work, while culture is about how people behave and how systems reinforce or discourage those behaviors.

To create inclusive workplaces, we must shift from short-term DEI (diversity, equity, and inclusion) programming to long-term cultural engineering—building trust, modeling fairness, and designing systems that enable every employee to thrive.

The Equitable Excellence™ Framework: Where Equity and Performance Are Not in Competition, But in Concert

To help organizations move from aspiration to action, I developed the **Equitable Excellence™ Framework**—a cultural model that integrates the strengths of both DEI (diversity, equity, and inclusion) and MEI (merit, excellence, and intelligence, a concept coined by Alexandr Wang, CEO of Scale AI).

Rather than viewing equity and performance as competing goals, Equitable Excellence aligns them. It offers a path for operationalizing fairness and high performance through five core strategies. These strategies are not theoretical ideals—they are activated through intentional practices that reinforce your organization's people strategy across the employee lifecycle.

Aligned Leadership Behaviors

Leaders must model equity and excellence—not just preach it.

Activation Practices:

- Define inclusive behaviors as part of core leadership competencies.
- Train leaders to listen actively, foster psychological safety, and value diverse perspectives.
- Hold leaders accountable for building equitable, high-performing teams.
- Reward collaboration alongside individual outcomes.

Embedded Equity in Decision-Making

Fairness must be designed into your processes—not left to chance.

Activation Practices:

- Audit pay equity, promotion pathways, and access to development.
- Remove unintentional barriers embedded in legacy systems and policies.
- Implement 360-degree feedback to reduce subjectivity in evaluations.
- Use transparent, outcomes-based performance standards tied to values.

Role Clarity with Flexibility

Clarity enables fairness. Flexibility enables adaptation.

Activation Practices:

- Apply structured interviews and skills-based assessments in hiring.
- Train hiring teams to recognize bias and evaluate potential fairly.
- Define clear performance and behavior expectations.
- Provide equitable access to flexible work and stretch assignments.

Transparent Growth Pathways

When employees can see a future, they stay and thrive.

Activation Practices:

- Build diverse talent pipelines and mentorship programs.
- Launch sponsorship initiatives for underrepresented groups.
- Clarify career progression and promotion criteria.
- Make development opportunities accessible beyond informal networks.

Feedback Loops that Reinforce Learning

Equity and excellence evolve. Learning must be continuous.

Activation Practices:

- Use data analytics to track advancement, retention, and inclusion sentiment.
- Conduct pulse surveys and behavior-focused feedback loops.
- Adapt strategies based on employee experience and feedback.
- Measure behaviors, not just beliefs, to assess culture alignment.

Why It Matters

The **Equitable Excellence™ Framework** allows organizations to center fairness without compromising performance. It provides a blueprint for building a people strategy where diversity is welcomed, inclusion is practiced, and excellence is the standard.

In too many organizations, equity initiatives live in one silo while performance management lives in another. Leaders are often forced to choose between creating a fair workplace or driving results. This is a false choice.

Equitable Excellence makes the case that equity and excellence are not in opposition—they are mutually reinforcing. High-performing organizations are not just diverse in who they hire; they are inclusive in how they lead. They create systems that enable all talent to contribute fully, grow meaningfully, and be recognized equitably.

These five core strategies are the ones that, in my experience, organizations most often neglect or struggle to implement. **Addressing them in a way that focuses on behaviors rather than bullet points is the distinguishing feature of the Equitable Excellence Framework.**

This is not about choosing between equity or performance. It's about choosing both—intentionally, strategically, and sustainably.

Belonging as a Cultural Outcome

When equity is embedded into systems and modeled by leaders, the result is belonging, a felt sense of psychological safety and inclusion. Belonging doesn't mean comfort; it means trust, agency, and the ability to contribute fully without fear of exclusion.

Belonging cannot be demanded—it must be designed, cultivated, and reinforced.

Case in Point: Moving from Metrics to Meaning

A national nonprofit invested heavily in DEI training and talent analytics but still faced high turnover among employees of color. After applying the Equitable Excellence Framework, they discovered gaps in mentorship, inconsistent performance evaluation practices, and unclear promotion pathways.

Through systemic changes—including inclusive leadership training, transparent evaluation rubrics, and a restructured development program—they shifted from measuring inclusion to enabling it.

Turnover dropped by 20%, but more importantly, internal surveys revealed a growing sense of trust and voice. One employee said, "I don't just feel represented—I feel respected."

Practitioner Reflection Points

- How is equity embedded into your leadership, evaluation, and hiring systems?
- Are inclusion efforts measured by outcomes—or by attendance at events?
- What structural barriers might exist in your organization that you haven't named yet?

Chapter 6 Summary

- Equity and excellence are not opposites. They are interdependent.
- Belonging results from a culture where people trust the systems and the people around them.
- The Equitable Excellence Framework provides a pathway to align fairness with performance.
- Leaders must model inclusive behavior and be held accountable for cultivating equity.
- Behavioral tools such as Culture15 allow organizations to measure how inclusion shows up in daily actions—not just policies.

Culture as Strategic Lever: From Soft Talk to Hard Results

Culture eats strategy for breakfast.
But aligned culture fuels strategy like
rocket fuel.

Culture is often dismissed as "the soft stuff." It's intangible, messy, and difficult to measure, and it's the hardest force to replicate. Yet research and real-world performance data tell us that culture is the most powerful driver of sustained success.

Organizations that treat culture as a strategic lever, rather than an HR initiative, outperform their peers in retention, innovation, and financial growth. The key is understanding that culture isn't separate from strategy—it is the context through which strategy is executed.

The Culture–Strategy Connection

Culture and strategy must move in tandem. Strategy sets direction; culture determines how people move in that direction—fast or slow, together or in silos, proactively or reactively.

When culture is misaligned with strategy, employees are unclear on priorities or don't feel safe acting on them. Risk-taking is punished, even when innovation has been named as a priority. The result is that great ideas get stalled in bureaucracy.

When culture and strategy are aligned, leadership decisions reinforce the organization's goals. Teams act with clarity and confidence, and people even self-correct based on shared norms.

In short, strategy is what you plan to do, and culture is how it actually happens.

Making Culture a Strategic Asset

Organizations that treat culture strategically do four things well. Here's how to become such an organization:

1. Define the Culture Needed for Strategic Success

Rather than generic values, identify the specific behaviors and mindsets your strategy requires. If innovation is key, what behaviors will support it? If scale and consistency are your focus, what routines should matter most?

2. Measure the Culture as It Actually Exists

Move beyond engagement scores and sentiment surveys by using behavior-based assessments. These tools help reveal patterns in how people interact, make decisions, and navigate systems—shining light on where culture accelerates or inhibits strategic goals.

3. Close the Gap Through Targeted Interventions

Once the gap is clear, work with leadership to redesign systems and incentives so that they reflect the organization's priorities. Adjust leadership behavior through coaching. Create storytelling and feedback loops to reinforce change. These focused strategies will close the gap between strategy and culture.

4. Build Culture Accountability into Strategic Reviews

If we truly believe that culture drives outcomes, then we must treat it with the same discipline and visibility we apply to financials or KPIs. A *Culture Scorecard* makes that possible. It helps leaders track the behavioral, relational, and trust-building elements that fuel performance—so they're not left to assumption or anecdote.

Below is a sample Culture Scorecard aligned with the principles of behavioral accountability, equity, and organizational health:

The Culture Scorecard

Focus Area	What to Measure	How to Measure It	How Often	Why It Matters
Behavioral Alignment	Are values showing up in everyday actions?	360° reviews, pulse checks, behavioral assessments	Quarterly	Shows whether culture is lived, not just laminated.
Psychological Safety	Do employees feel safe to speak up and take risks?	Inclusion index, safety surveys, focus groups	Biannually	Essential for innovation, retention, and trust.
Leadership Modeling	Are leaders consistently demonstrating core behaviors?	Upward feedback, peer ratings, team sentiment data	Quarterly	Culture follows what leadership models—not what it says.

Focus Area	What to Measure	How to Measure It	How Often	Why It Matters
Equity in Opportunity	Is access to advancement truly equitable?	Promotion data, representation tracking	Annually	Reinforces fairness and signals structural alignment.
Trust in Decisions	Are decisions made with clarity and inclusion?	Employee surveys, decision audits	Quarterly	Builds ownership and reduces resistance to change.
Collaboration and Agility	Are teams working across silos and adapting effectively?	Project retrospectives, collaboration metrics	Biannually	Culture must support adaptability, not reinforce rigidity.

Culture Isn't a Monolith

Strategic cultures aren't about being "nice" or "fun." They're about being aligned, intentional, and performance-ready. A strategic culture is one that is deliberately shaped to support your business goals—it's not aspirational fluff, it's operational fuel.

And here's the truth: Most organizations don't have one single culture. They have multiple subcultures that reflect the realities of different teams, functions, or geographies. That's not a flaw; it's a feature—if you manage it well.

You might see:

- High-speed decision-making in one business unit
- Thoughtful consensus-building in another
- Formality and process in highly regulated environments
- Bold experimentation in innovation teams

The right culture is the one that helps your strategy win. But it doesn't happen by accident.

Case in Point: Culture Drives Strategic Agility

A global manufacturing company launched an ambitious five-year digital transformation strategy. Despite investments in technology, results lagged. Employees hesitated to adopt new tools, middle managers defaulted to old ways of working, and decision-making remained siloed.

A cultural assessment revealed that the company's long-standing "risk-avoidant" mindset conflicted with its new innovation-driven strategy. Leaders decided to name the issue publicly and build a new set of strategic behaviors into performance goals: curiosity, responsiveness, and cross-functional collaboration.

With coaching, behavior modeling, and recognition programs, teams slowly began embracing experimentation. Within eighteen months, digital tool adoption soared and customer satisfaction increased. Culture had been the missing link in strategy execution.

Practitioner Reflection Points

- Does your culture enable or block your current strategy?
- Are you measuring cultural behaviors—not just values or engagement?
- What habits or rituals could be shifted to better align with your strategic goals?

Chapter 7 Summary

- Culture is not separate from strategy—it shapes how strategy is lived.
- A culture that is misaligned with strategy slows progress and breeds resistance.
- Measuring real behaviors enables intentional cultural shifts.
- Strategic cultures are designed, reinforced, and reviewed just like any other business asset.
- When culture and strategy move in tandem, organizational performance accelerates.

Measuring What Matters: Making the Intangible Actionable

You can't manage what you don't measure—but you also can't lead what you don't understand.

One of the biggest myths in organizational life is that culture, behavior, and trust can't be measured. As a result, many leaders default to what's easiest to quantify: revenue, head count, attrition, or survey satisfaction scores. But these tell only part of the story—and often they are the indicators that lag the most.

If you want to drive real, lasting transformation, you must be willing to measure what truly matters—even if it's difficult. That includes leadership behavior, values alignment, trust, adaptability, and psychological safety.

From Output Metrics to Behavioral Indicators

Traditional performance metrics track *what* gets done, based on outputs like financials, turnover, and task completion. But sustainable performance depends on *how* work gets done. Behavioral indicators help you assess:

- How decisions are made (independently or through consensus)
- Whether leaders model core values
- How conflict is navigated
- How transparently information is shared
- If people feel safe to speak up or take risks
- Whether new ideas are encouraged—or quietly shut down

Behaviors are the leading indicators of culture, engagement, and long-term resilience.

What to Measure—and How

To measure the right things, organizations must track performance across behavioral, relational, and cultural dimensions—not just output.

Focus Area	Sample Metrics
Behavioral alignment	360° feedback, team charters, values-based performance reviews
Trust and safety	Psychological safety pulse checks, conflict escalation data
Leadership modeling	Peer or upward feedback, coaching impact scores
Inclusion and belonging	Sentiment analysis, exit interviews, belonging index
Agility and adaptability	Change readiness assessments, innovation pipeline tracking

Use a mix of quantitative and qualitative tools. Numbers will reveal patterns. Stories will reveal truth.

Making the Intangible Visible

Culture is not a soft concept. It's simply a set of behavioral realities that become measurable when you pay attention to:

- What people consistently do
- What leaders reward—or ignore
- Where resistance shows up
- Where voice is encouraged—or silenced

One way organizations begin this work is by using internal culture diagnostics, structured interviews, or pulse tools that track behavioral norms. These tools help teams see not just how people feel but how they act. When aligned to your strategy, this behavioral intelligence becomes actionable insight.

The best tools aren't necessarily the most complex. They're the ones your organization will actually use—and, more importantly, the ones your people will trust. Whether it's a formal platform or a well-designed internal process, what matters most is measuring what matters—and making it matter.

Case in Point: When Innovation Stalled

A midsized tech startup had gained early traction in the market with a strong product and a mission-driven team. But as the company scaled, the CEO noticed a troubling pattern: product releases were getting delayed, tensions across departments were increasing, and innovation had slowed to a crawl.

Traditional engagement surveys suggested that employees were generally satisfied, but the data didn't explain the bottlenecks. The leadership team commissioned a behavioral culture audit focused on decision-making, collaboration, and psychological safety.

What they found was telling:

- Teams were unclear on decision rights and accountability.

- Junior staff hesitated to challenge ideas or speak up.

- Collaboration was cautious, defaulting to consensus rather than progress.

Armed with these insights, the company made targeted changes:

- Clarified decision authority across functions.

- Trained managers in conflict fluency and constructive dissent.

- Created space in team stand-ups for raising red flags and pitching bold ideas.

Within six months, product cycle time improved by 22%, and internal pulse surveys showed a significant uptick in perceived innovation climate.

By measuring behavior, not just mood, they uncovered the invisible friction slowing their growth and reoriented the culture around clarity, trust, and speed.

The Role of Curiosity in Measuring What Matters

In working with organizations in various industries, one of the most overlooked leadership traits I've observed in culture transformation work is curiosity. When we talk about measurement—especially of things like trust, behavior, or alignment—it's easy to focus on the numbers and miss the nuances. But curiosity changes that.

Curiosity invites us to ask deeper questions—not just what is happening, but why. It's what turns data into insight. When leaders review engagement scores or behavioral assessments with a curious mindset, they shift from a place of judgment to one of understanding. They stop asking "Who's to blame?" and start asking "What are we learning?"

This is where real culture work begins.

Curiosity also helps bring to the surface things data alone can't always reveal: context, motivation, and lived experience. Curiosity builds trust because it says, "I want to understand before I act." That's a leadership behavior worth measuring, too.

Practitioner Reflection Points

- Are your metrics telling you what's working—or just what's visible?
- What behaviors are rewarded in your culture, intentionally or not?
- Are you measuring belonging, safety, and trust—or assuming them?
- What is your system for checking leadership behavior and its alignment with culture?
- What story is your data trying to tell you and are you willing to listen without jumping to conclusions?

Chapter 8 Summary

- You can measure culture—it just requires focusing on behavior rather than sentiment.
- Leading organizations track alignment, inclusion, adaptability, and trust as well as performance.
- Tools and dashboards are only as effective as the conversations they spark.
- Metrics should drive curiosity, not compliance.
- When you measure what matters, you can lead with clarity and confidence.

Building a Sustainable People Strategy

Your people strategy isn't separate from your business strategy. It's how your business strategy comes to life.

Most organizations recognize that talent is their most important asset. Fewer treat it as a strategic advantage. Fewer still build the internal systems needed to manage it sustainably.

A sustainable people strategy ensures that your approaches to culture, talent, and leadership are designed to scale alongside your goals—not chase them reactively. It aligns operations with values. It embeds equity into systems. And it creates a blueprint for leading through change, not just surviving it.

What Makes a People Strategy Sustainable?

Sustainability in the people space means more than minimizing burnout or improving retention. It means designing a culture and talent system that can adapt, grow, and regenerate over time. Key characteristics include:

- **Strategic integration.** The people strategy is co-developed with business strategy, not after the fact.
- **Values in action.** Organizational values are embedded in hiring, onboarding, performance, and rewards.
- **Continuous focus on behavior.** Leaders are developed, aligned, and evaluated based on cultural and business behaviors.
- **Equity by design.** Barriers are identified and dismantled through systems thinking—not as reactive fixes.
- **Data-driven learning.** Metrics guide not just decisions but learning loops across the organization.

The Pillars of a Sustainable People Strategy

1. Purpose and Values Alignment

A sustainable people strategy starts with connecting mission, vision, and values to how work is done every day. This provides employees with meaning, clarity, and a shared North Star.

We hire for skill and mindset, but we keep people because they embody our values. That kind of alignment doesn't happen by accident—it's taught, reinforced, and led from the top.

2. Leadership Development as a Cultural Lever

A sustainable people strategy treats leadership not just as a role but as a responsibility for shaping the environment. Accordingly, leadership agrees on a set of leadership behaviors aligned with culture and performance. They reinforce these behaviors through coaching, peer feedback, and accountability structures. And they ensure new leaders are not just technically prepared, but culturally ready.

3. Systemic Equity Integration

A sustainable people strategy uses the Equitable Excellence Framework as a foundation for integrating fairness into each part of the employee life cycle. These include hiring and onboarding processes; performance and development reviews; and advancement, mobility, and retention efforts. This ensures that talent systems amplify both equity and excellence rather than force a trade-off between them.

4. Workforce Agility and Capability Building

A sustainable people strategy equips an organization to adapt and thrive in changing conditions. It does this by creating systems that support cross-functional skill development, foster a culture of learning by rewarding curiosity, and establish clear roles that still allow for flexibility. An example would be a rotational program that gives employees exposure to multiple departments—strengthening collaboration and broadening organizational awareness.

In high-performing organizations, learning is continuous, curiosity is encouraged, and structure exists but never becomes rigidity. Agile organizations don't just react; they reconfigure in response to change.

5. Culture as an Operating Model

A sustainable people strategy reflects the understanding that culture isn't a destination—it's a design choice. It uses culture as a lens for decision-making, keeping an intentional focus on these questions:

- How do we resolve tension and conflict?
- How do we celebrate progress?
- How do we adapt, include, and listen?

These daily decisions define your real operating model.

Case in Point: Embedding Culture in the Operating Model

A national organization undergoing leadership turnover and shifting workforce expectations recognized the need to move from reactive HR tactics to a unified, people-centered strategy. While their mission was clear, their internal culture was inconsistent—driven more by personalities than by shared values.

Through the application of the Equitable Excellence framework, I partnered with the organization's entire leadership structure—from frontline supervisors to the president—to co-create a strategic people model. A critical component of this effort was establishing a unified communication flow that ensured clarity, consistency, and transparency across all levels. This, combined with a focus on aligning leadership behaviors, standardizing development opportunities, and embedding equity into daily decisions, created a strong foundation for cultural alignment.

The initiative included quarterly facilitated working sessions to define core leadership expectations, peer coaching to reinforce inclusive practices, and recalibrated performance conversations tied to both outcomes and behaviors. Managers were equipped with tools to recognize contributions equitably, share information openly, and model mission-aligned behavior with consistency.

In just over a year, the organization reported measurable improvements in team cohesion, talent retention, and psychological safety. More importantly, leaders across levels began to see culture not as a separate initiative, but as an operating model—one that empowered them to lead with clarity, equity, and intention.

Practitioner Reflection Points

- Is your people strategy proactive—or patchwork?
- How well do your talent practices reflect your mission and values?
- Are you building leadership and equity for the future— or just filling roles for today?

Chapter 9 Summary

- A sustainable people strategy aligns culture, leadership, and operations with business priorities.
- Equity, adaptability, and values activation must be designed into systems—not left to chance.
- Leadership behavior is both the catalyst and the guardian of culture.
- Tools like Culture15 and the Equitable Excellence Framework make the intangible visible—and actionable.
- Sustainable strategies regenerate the workforce while fueling performance.

CHAPTER 10

What's Next: Taking the First Step Toward Sustainable Transformation

You've reached the end of this book, but this is where the real work begins.

Human capital transformation is not a one-time effort. It's a continuous, evolving commitment to put people at the center of the systems, strategies, and decisions that define your organization.

So what's next? That depends on where you are in your journey. Whether you're a leader seeking clarity, an HR professional ready to shift your role, or a consultant guiding organizations toward alignment—there's always a next step.

I recommend starting with these three actions:

1. Reflect

Ask yourself:

- What behaviors do I reinforce in my team, intentionally or unintentionally?
- Where is our culture misaligned with our stated values?
- Are our systems designed for compliance—or for growth?

Clarity begins with honest reflection. Take time to assess where your influence can have the greatest impact.

2. Facilitate One Conversation That Matters

Transformation doesn't have to start with a restructure. It can begin with one real conversation—about expectations, trust, decision-making, or accountability.

Invite your team to explore:

- What's working?
- What's missing?
- What do we want to see more of?

Sometimes, momentum starts with naming what's already in the room.

3. Identify Practices You Can Start Tomorrow

Start putting ideas into practice. Some suggestions:

- Clarify one behavioral expectation for your team and start reinforcing it consistently.
- Schedule a real-time alignment conversation with a peer leader to compare how values show up in daily decisions.
- Audit your team's performance conversations. Are they focused only on results, or also on how work is done?
- Model one courageous behavior you want others to embrace—such as candid, growth-focused feedback, conflict navigation, or transparency.
- Acknowledge one behavior in someone else that aligns with your desired culture. Make your acknowledgment visible and specific.

Small actions compound. Culture grows where leadership behaves on purpose.

Use This Book as a Shared Resource

When you are ready to share the ideas in this book more widely, choose a chapter that speaks to your current challenge and use it to spark dialogue in your next leadership meeting, coaching session, or team retreat.

Each chapter was written to stand alone—and to support collective learning. If you're not sure where to begin, chapters 2 and 5 are excellent entry points.

About Appendixes I and II

Appendix I contains summaries of the eight frameworks and models introduced in this book. Use it to reinforce key concepts, revisit core strategies, and quickly reference the tools that support implementation. Whether you're facilitating a leadership session, designing a culture initiative, or coaching a team, this appendix serves as a practical guide to apply the insights from each chapter in real time. Appendix II lists tools and books for your continuous growth.

Build Forward—With People at the Center

This book started with a simple truth: people are not just your greatest asset, they are the foundation of everything your organization does and everything it can become.

Throughout these pages, we've explored what it means to move beyond transactional HR, beyond performative culture, beyond fragmented leadership—to something deeper, more enduring, and more powerful: a people strategy that drives sustainable transformation.

- We've named the behaviors that shape performance.
- We've called attention to the systems that reinforce accountability.

- We've challenged the notion that engagement is enough without a culture that actually supports it.
- We've clarified how leadership, equity, and adaptability must be built into the day-to-day—not treated as side projects.
- And we've elevated the role of HR—not to fix what's broken, but to build what's next.

This is not just a framework. It's a call:

- A call to make human capital not merely a department but a lens.
- A call to rethink the way your organization defines value and success.
- A call to step into the next level of leadership—not with more control but with more clarity, connection, and courage.

You don't need to do everything at once. Start with what's possible. Maybe it's one conversation. One shift in how feedback is given. One effort to align your team. One system redesigned with purpose.

Because when we invest in our people—their behavior, their growth, their leadership—we don't just improve the workplace. We unlock the future.

A Letter to the Future of Work

Dear Reader,

Thank you for walking this journey with me. You didn't just read this book about human capital—you invested your time and thought in reimagining what human capital could mean.

Looking ahead, I believe the most resilient organizations will be those that choose to humanize the way they operate, even as the world around them digitizes. That means aligning systems and strategy with how people learn, grow, and thrive—at every level.

In my |TEDx| talk, "Humanizing AI: The Role of P.E.O.P.L.E. in Digital Transformation," I explored what it truly means to build a future of work that doesn't sacrifice humanity for efficiency. That vision is possible, but it takes intention, leadership, and aligned behaviors across the employee lifecycle.

You hold the power to shape that future. The models in this book are just a starting point. The transformation begins when you choose to lead it.

Stay bold. Stay intentional. And above all—stay human.

Warmly,
Daphne

The 8 Actionable Frameworks

This appendix summarizes the eight models and frameworks introduced in this book. Each is designed to help leaders, HR professionals, and teams translate theory into practice as they align people strategy with business performance.

1. The Human Capital Flow Model™

- Maps the evolution of HR from a transactional function to a strategic enabler
- Aligns HR's value across the employee life cycle:

Phase	Focus Area	Key Outcomes
Anchor	Operational Excellence	Compliance, stability, trust
Align	Strategic Behavior and Culture	Role clarity, performance, engagement
Accelerate	Organizational Agility and Talent Optimization	Innovation, transformation, growth

- **Application:** Use the ***Human Capital Flow Model*** to assess where your HR function spends its energy, and where it needs to shift to meet future demands.

ORGANIZATIONAL AGILITY &TALENT OPTIMIZATION

KEY OUTCOMES:
• INNOVATION
• TRANSFORMATION
• GROWTH

ACCELERATE

STRATEGIC BEHAVIOR & CULTURE

KEY OUTCOMES:
• ROLE CLARITY
• PERFORMANCE
• ENGAGEMENT

ALIGN

OPERATIONAL EXCELLENCE

KEY OUTCOMES:
• COMPLIANCE
• STABILITY
• TRUST

ANCHOR

DBL

2. The Equitable Excellence™ Framework

- Bridges diversity, equity, and inclusion (DEI) with merit, excellence, and intelligence (MEI), creating a high-trust, high-performance culture
- Five core practices:

  » **Equitable Hiring**—objective selection with diverse sourcing

  » **Inclusive Leadership**—modeling equity, psychological safety, and diverse thinking

  » **Transparent Evaluation**—clear performance standards aligned with strategy

  » **Access to Development**—equitable learning and mentorship opportunities

  » **Organizational Accountability**—data-driven tracking of equity and outcomes

- **Application:** Use the *Equitable Excellence Framework* to conduct equity audits, guide leadership behaviors, or redesign talent systems for both fairness and performance.

3. The Behavior-to-Business-Results Loop™

- Shows how individual behaviors, when supported by systems and expectations, create self-reinforcing results
- Loop progression:

  Behavior → Systems → Culture → Results → Reinforcement → Behavior

- **Application:** Diagnose gaps where desired outcomes are not aligned with culture or behaviors. For example, is innovation rewarded? Is accountability modeled?

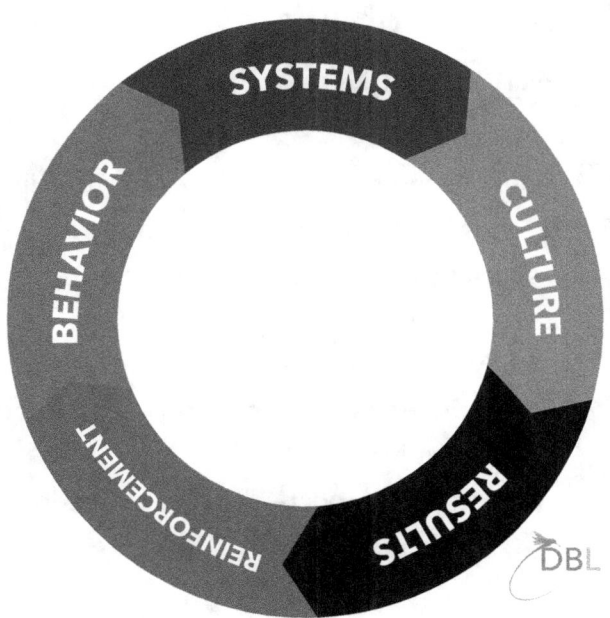

4. The Accountability Alignment Triangle™

- A simple diagnostic for performance ownership
- Helps ensure work is clearly owned, behaviors are defined, and systems support consistent execution
- Three elements:
    - o **Role Clarity**—What am I accountable for?
    - o **Behavioral Expectations**—How should I deliver it?
    - o **System Support**—Do rewards, feedback, and tools reinforce this?

- **Application:** Use the *Accountability Alignment Triangle* as a coaching or performance development tool during one-to-ones, team planning, or leadership alignment sessions.

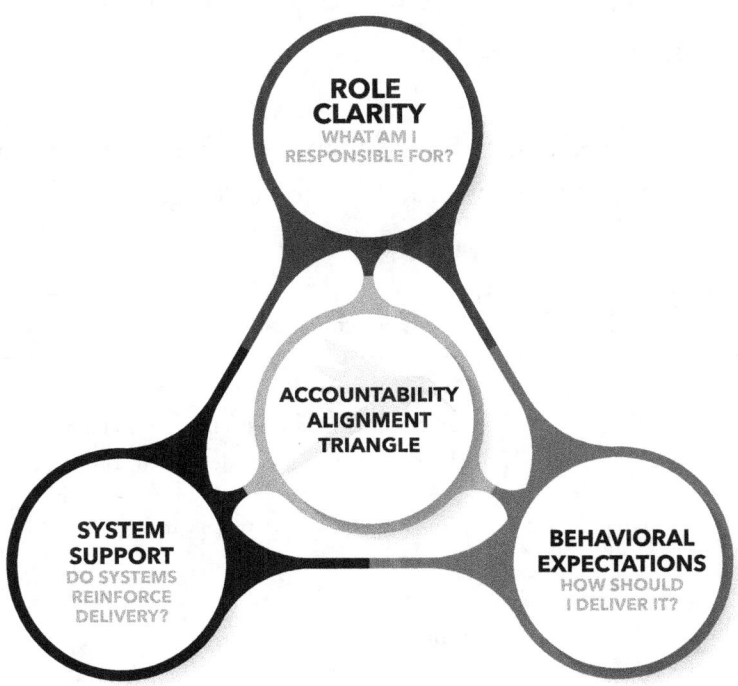

5. The Culture Design Lens Maps organizational culture so it can be shaped by design

- Breaks organizational culture into five observable domains of behavior and decision-making:

Focus Area	Key Questions
People Dynamics	Are individuals empowered to contribute meaningfully? Do team members challenge ideas constructively or default to conformity?
Motivation & Drive	Does our culture encourage innovation and bold thinking, or do we default to safety and predictability? What truly inspires our teams?
Communication Flow	Is information transparent and accessible across levels? Do our systems support open dialogue or reinforce silos?

Focus Area	Key Questions
Decision-Making	Are decisions inclusive and aligned with our values—or driven primarily by hierarchy and urgency? How consistent is our approach?
Execution Rhythm	Do we balance strategic planning with agility? How open are we to new ideas and adaptive ways of working?

- **Application:** Use the *Culture Design Lens* as a team diagnostic or retreat tool to assess how your stated values align with lived behaviors.

6. The Leadership Flow™ Map

- Enables distributed leadership in real time
- Helps operationalize leadership beyond the title—especially at the team and mid-manager level
- Key practices:
  - o **Micro-Decisions**—to encourage daily ownership and initiative
  - o **Coaching Conversations**—making feedback a two-way norm
  - o **Feedback Loops**—creating rituals for learning in real time
  - o **Real-Time Alignment**—staying centered on purpose and shared goals
  - o **Safe Experimentation**—reducing fear of failure to increase agility
- **Application:** Use the *Leadership Flow Map* to train managers to lead in the moment, not just from the meeting room. Reinforce this model during onboarding, agile planning, and project launches.

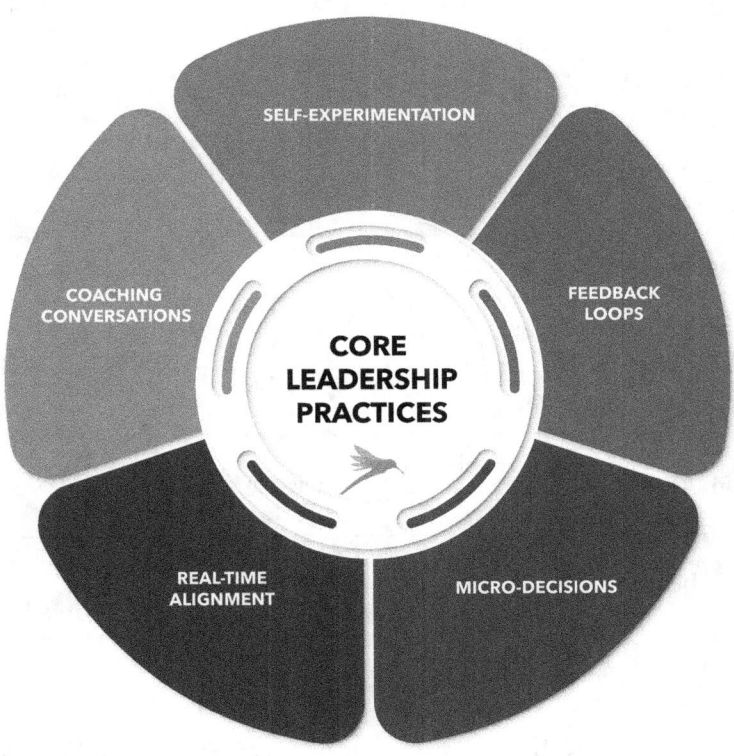

7. The Change Capability Continuum™

- Describes the shift from reactive change to strategic adaptability
- Helps organizations evolve to treat change as a built-in capability rather than a disruption:

Stage	Characteristics	Risks	Opportunities
Reactive	Change = threat; decisions are top-down	Low trust, high resistance	Short-term fixes
Managed	Change = planned event with support	Change fatigue	Moderate resilience
Embedded	Change = strategic capability	High agility	Innovation, competitive edge

- **Application:** Use the *Change Capability Continuum* to assess where your organization currently stands and to identify where leader and team capabilities must evolve.

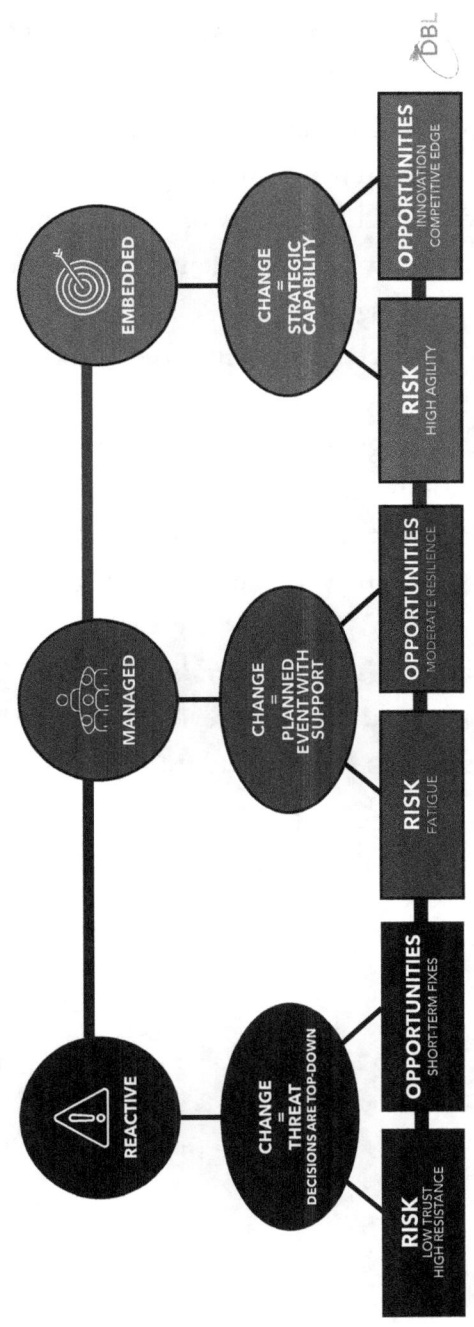

8. The Leadership Behavior Compass™

- Aids in defining and modeling core leadership behaviors observed in high-performing organizations
- Maps four directional behaviors leaders must master:
  - o **Clarity**—setting vision, defining expectations, reducing ambiguity
  - o **Connection**—building trust, showing empathy, creating inclusion
  - o **Courage**—naming conflict, making hard calls, leading through uncertainty
  - o **Consistency**—reinforcing behaviors, maintaining alignment, following through

- **Application:** Use the *Leadership Behavior Compass* in executive coaching, 360° reviews, or leadership team charters to align on expectations.

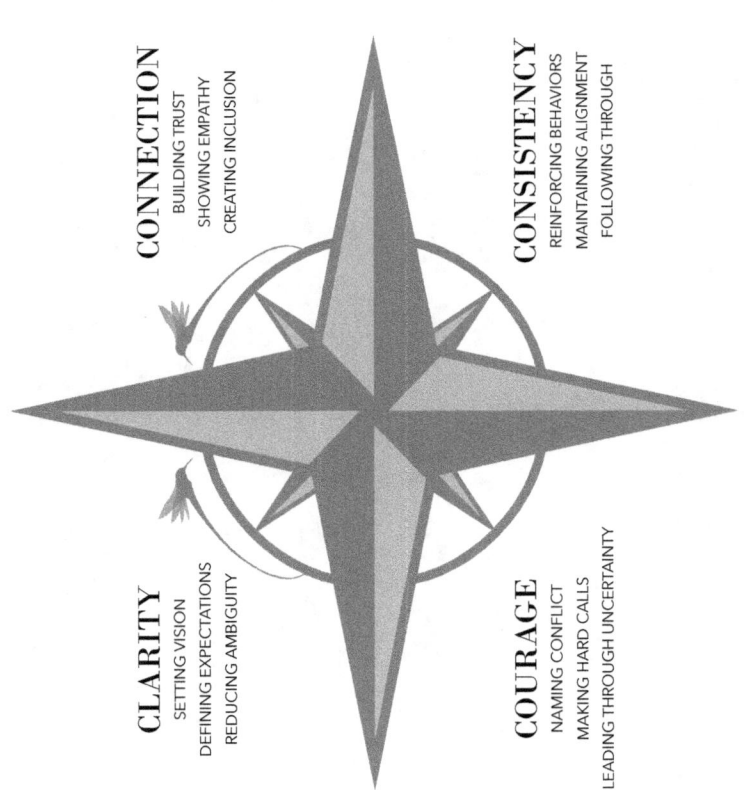

CONNECTION
BUILDING TRUST
SHOWING EMPATHY
CREATING INCLUSION

CONSISTENCY
REINFORCING BEHAVIORS
MAINTAINING ALIGNMENT
FOLLOWING THROUGH

CLARITY
SETTING VISION
DEFINING EXPECTATIONS
REDUCING AMBIGUITY

COURAGE
NAMING CONFLICT
MAKING HARD CALLS
LEADING THROUGH UNCERTAINTY

Resources for Continued Growth

Below are resources—some conceptual, some practical—to help you as you move forward.

Recommended Tools

- **Culture15**—A platform to define, design, and drive organizational culture through leadership behaviors.
  Contact: https://culture15.com

- **Equitable Excellence™ Framework**—Developed to help organizations embed equity into performance systems and culture.
  Contact: https://daphneblatimore.com

- **Tilt 365 Profile**—A strength-based personality tool useful for coaching and team dynamics.
  Contact: https://www.tilt365.com

- **360° feedback platforms**—To capture diverse perspectives on leadership behaviors in real time. Many such platforms are available; search online for them or ask me for recommendations.

Recommended Books

- *Drive: The Surprising Truth About What Motivates Us* by Daniel Pink
- *The Fearless Organization: Creating Psychological Safety in the Workplace for Learning, Innovation, and Growth* by Amy Edmondson
- *Reinventing Organizations* by Frederic Laloux
- *Braving the Wilderness* by Brené Brown

A Message from Daphne

I'm Daphne B. Latimore, SPHR, HCS, CEC—an organizational strategist and author of the leadership trilogy Human Capital at the Core, You Should Be a Coach, and The Power of Presence. For more than 30 years, I've helped leaders across industries turn complexity into clarity by aligning culture, leadership behaviors, and business systems.

My work centers on translating values into action and positioning people strategy at the heart of business transformation. I believe that when coaching presence, strategic clarity, and human energy flow with intention, performance follows, and organizations thrive.

If you're ready to bring this work into your organization, I'd love to be part of your journey.

Let's explore how we can:

- Facilitate leadership alignment sessions
- Co-design a human capital strategy
- Train your team to lead behavior, not just performance
- Embed the Equitable Excellence™ framework into your culture

You can reach out at:
https://www.dblatimore.com

Or connect via LinkedIn:
https://www.linkedin.com/in/daphneblatimore

Change doesn't happen just because we finish a book.

It happens when we turn insight into action, and lead with greater clarity, courage, and intention.

You've done the work of reading. Now, it's time to lead differently.
Your people are watching.
Your mission is calling.
And the future of work won't wait.

Let's build what comes next—on purpose.

Full Reviews

"This book is an excellent reference/guidebook for leadership in any size organization. I found myself taking notes and wanting to apply the concepts to my business from the very first chapter.

The book captures and quantifies the elusive measure of human capital. I could clearly see the link and all too often the missing link to traditional strategy and measure that often falls short in building a company's human capital.

The book was a quick and easy read. Each chapter can stand alone and apply to a business overall or to different segments of a business. I will be recommending this book to my clients, from start up businesses to companies that are seasoned and successful."
—**Douglas M. Marshall,** III CPA

"I first met Daphne Latimore as a brilliant facilitator who supported our team to connect more honestly. In this book, as in that powerful experience, Daphne diagnoses the reality beneath the surface of organizational life; she prompts leaders to bring their divergent styles and views out into the open so they can tackle conflict directly and reach alignment; and she demonstrates how equity and top performance are mutually reinforcing values. Above all, she gently yet persistently pushes leaders never to stop at just saying the right thing but rather always to stay the course till they are doing it."
—**Dr. Olivia A. Golden,** former nonprofit ED and senior public sector leader

www.ingramcontent.com/pod-product-compliance
Lightning Source LLC
Chambersburg PA
CBHW071338130626
46556CB00004B/1932